RABBITS

Other titles in the series

Keeping and Caring for Your Pet

Fish: Keeping and Caring for Your Pet
Library Edition ISBN 978-0-7660-4185-1
Paperback ISBN 978-1-4644-0301-9

Guinea Pigs: Keeping and Caring for Your Pet
Library Edition ISBN 978-0-7660-4184-4
Paperback ISBN 978-1-4644-0299-9

Kittens: Keeping and Caring for Your Pet
Library Edition ISBN 978-0-7660-4186-8
Paperback ISBN 978-1-4644-0303-3

Puppies: Keeping and Caring for Your Pet
Library Edition ISBN 978-0-7660-4187-5
Paperback ISBN 978-1-4644-0305-7

RABBITS

Keeping and
Caring for
Your Pet

Angela Beck

Enslow Publishers, Inc.
40 Industrial Road
Box 398
Berkeley Heights, NJ 07922
USA

http://www.enslow.com

Contents

1

2

3

1

Choosing and Bringing Home a Rabbit

A Journey Into the Wild

Somewhere in Europe, on a sandy plain, it is nearly dusk with grass and bushes as far as the eye can see. If you take a closer look, you will notice the ground resembles Swiss cheese. There are holes everywhere, entrances and exits. Under cover of dusk there is a creature nibbling and hopping around . . . it is a wild rabbit!

Wild Rabbits

Wild rabbits are very sociable and live in extended families in self-dug burrows. They are true architects who create numerous tunnels, main entrances, residential areas, and emergency exits. They prefer their habitats to be hilly and covered with bushes, with a sandy ground if possible, which provides plenty of protection and also food.

Order, Not Chaos

Rabbits are very neat and tidy animals. They have their own special areas to go to the bathroom outside their burrows. Also, the main entrances are always kept open and clean, while the emergency exits are well hidden underneath bushes.

Always on the Run

Since rabbits have many natural enemies that would chase them for miles if given the chance, they have to live very carefully. They do not usually leave their burrows to search for food unless they are under the protection of the dim light of dawn or dusk. They remain vigilant at all times. They use their eyes, ears, and nose to explore their environment and are always ready to run at a moment's notice.

Jungle Drums

As soon as something suspicious has been detected, the rabbit will give an alarm signal. He uses his hind legs to drum on the ground, and suddenly all nearby rabbits disappear in the blink of an eye, as if the ground had swallowed them up. This is what the emergency entrance is for.

Family Life

Rabbit babies are altricial animals, meaning they are born helpless, blind, and without any fur. They spend the first part of their lives being cared for by their mother. There is a fixed hierarchy within a wild rabbit family. A buck dominates over the males, and the female rabbit, called a doe, looks after the young. Rabbits use body language and scent to communicate with each other.

The Hare

Hares and rabbits are not the same animals. Hares live above ground and are loners. These shy wild animals prefer open areas, fields, meadows, and forest edges as their habitat. Their homes are very simple; they live in holes, in which they sit and sleep. With their brown coats and long ears pressed to their heads, they blend into their surroundings perfectly and can see everything around them. If something gets too close to them, they

Rabbits are very social animals. They live in large families in rabbit warrens, where they raise their young.

flee. With their long legs, they are perfect sprinters and can reach a speed of up to about fifty miles per hour. Hares also prefer to look for food in the twilight.

Mating Season

During the mating season, some hares shy away from the habitat because things can get out of hand. Bucks will fight over a doe, punching and kicking each other. The buck also runs the risk of being kicked by the doe if she does not want to mate. Unlike rabbits, baby hares are precocial animals, meaning they are born fully developed, with fur, and can fend for themselves soon after birth.

Hares are solitary animals. Their most obvious feature is their long ears, which can pick up almost any sound.

How Rabbits Became Pets

The Romans kept wild rabbits, mainly for food.

Fact File

Dwarf Rabbit

→ relatively short (about 2–3 inches), narrow ears that sit close together on the head

→ compact, rounded, squat body; body height and width approximately one-third of the body length

→ round, prominent head with broad forehead and nose and pronounced cheeks

→ weight: 2–3 pounds for a full-grown dwarf rabbit; up to 4 pounds for dwarf lop breeds

According to scientists, humans have been aware of the rabbit's existence since 1100 B.C., in what is now Spain and Portugal. About a thousand years later, the Romans developed a taste for them and brought them to Rome, where they were kept in fenced-in pens and bred for food.

Down Under–Rabbits Can Survive Almost Anywhere

Because rabbits are very adaptable and can survive almost anywhere, they have spread out in all directions, partly of their own accord, and partly by human intervention. Some even made it to Australia because an Englishman who had emigrated wanted to bring as much of his "home" with him as possible, and this included wild rabbits. Rabbits live very well in Australia, enjoy the habitat, and have no natural enemies, so they spread like wildfire. In places such as the United States, one can only wonder at their incredible adaptability: many rabbits live in the suburbs very close to humans.

From Wild Animal to Domestic Pet

All domestic rabbit breeds were developed from the European rabbit. Because rabbits could be found almost everywhere, it was not long before they were kept by humans and bred in captivity. They were valuable for their meat and fur.

The First Dwarf Rabbits

Over time, rabbits were bred selectively. The initial aim was to breed rabbits that were large with lots of meat and plenty of thick fur. Then they were bred for sport, which was a specialty of the Dutch and the English. The first known dwarf rabbit breed originated in England and was mentioned in nineteenth-century rabbit-raising books. This small rabbit had white fur and red eyes and was known as the Polish in England and as the Hermelin in Germany. (According to the American Rabbit Breeders Association, the rabbit currently known as the Polish here in the United States is different from the English breed of the same name. The rabbit known as the Polish in England was renamed the Britannia Petite in the United States.) In 1938, the Dutch rabbit breeder Minheer Hoefman bred a Hermelin rabbit with a wild rabbit and the result was the first-ever Netherland dwarf rabbit. With their rounded heads, large eyes, upturned noses, soft fur, and tame natures, dwarf rabbits quickly became popular with people of all ages.

Dwarf Rabbits As Pets

With their cute appearance, small size, and friendly nature, dwarf rabbits are one of the most popular pets. Children, in particular, take these rabbits very quickly into their hearts. Unfortunately, this is not always a good thing for the rabbit. Because they are so sweet and relatively inexpensive, they are often purchased as surprise presents, especially at Easter time. The recipient of the unwanted gift may be too busy or uninterested in the rabbit, so the poor animal has to spend most of his time alone in his cage. This is an absolute no-no for a rabbit! This book will show you how you can increase your rabbit's well-being by keeping him busy, as well as how to care for him and make him part of your family. This makes life with your rabbit fun!

Dwarf rabbit on the move! This dwarf rabbit is incredibly curious and investigates everything within his reach.

Rabbit Breeds

A glance in any pet shop will show you that dwarf rabbits are available in all shapes and colors: solid colors or spotted, long-haired or short-haired, erect ears or floppy ears. Generally, dwarf rabbits have relaxed, easygoing natures, which is part of what makes them so popular. Some dwarf rabbits are bred specifically to a predetermined standard; these rabbits have very specific characteristics and some are prizewinners at special shows.

There are many different breeds of dwarf rabbits, and the hybrid breeds are also just as appealing.

What Is a Dwarf Rabbit Breed?

The "dwarf rabbit" is not a specific breed in itself but rather an umbrella term that refers to all small rabbits. They usually weigh less than 4.5 pounds. Among the dwarf breeds are the Britannia Petite, Netherland dwarf, Jersey wooly, lionhead, mini rex, Holland lop, and American fuzzy lop.

Britannia Petite

With a maximum weight of 2.5 pounds, the Britannia Petite ties with the Netherland dwarf as the smallest breed of pet rabbit. The coat colors include black, black otter (black body with a lighter belly and chin), chestnut agouti (each hair has dark and light bands), sable marten (grayish brown coat with a lighter belly and chin), and white with red eyes. The rabbits with red eyes are albino.

Britannia Petites have wedge-shaped heads; large, round eyes; and short, erect ears close together. Their bodies are not round and stocky like the other dwarf breeds but more on the slender side.

Netherland Dwarf

The Netherland dwarf is widely recognized as the smallest breed of domestic rabbit, although its maximum weight is the same as the Britannia Petite's maximum. It was created by crossing red-eyed white Hermelins with other breeds to produce dwarf rabbits with different-colored coats. Color varieties include black, blue (blue-gray), red, Havana (dark brown), chinchilla, pearl, silver, sable, Siamese, Hotot (white with black around the eyes), and tan.

Jersey Wooly

The Rapunzel of the dwarf rabbit world is the Jersey wooly. The color varieties include pointed (white fur with darker fur on the nose, ears, feet, and tail), black, white, blue, chocolate, and lilac. Unlike an Angora rabbit, this long-haired dwarf does not need to be shorn, and it sheds no more fur than average.

Mini Rex

The mini rex is one of the larger dwarf breeds, with a maximum weight of 4.5 pounds. The coat of the mini rex is very short, about half an inch, very dense, and the hairs grow straight up. As a result, their fur feels very soft, just like velvet or silk. They come in a variety of different colors, including black, blue, white, chocolate, chinchilla, lilac, and red.

Holland Lop

Holland lops can be immediately identified by their large, floppy ears that hang down at the sides of the head. They have short, fluffy faces. Like the Netherland dwarf, the Holland lop is bred in all colors.

Lionhead

The lionhead rabbit is a relatively new breed in the United States and very popular. This rabbit has very long fur around her head that resembles a lion's mane. Some have two manes, one around the head and the other around the body. Long-haired breeds such as this require regular grooming.

American Fuzzy Lop

American fuzzy lops look like Holland lops but they have long, wooly fur on their heads and bodies. They are very social and playful. They enjoy being brushed if you start when the animals are young. This breed comes in many different colors, such as blue, black, pointed white, solid white, chocolate, chinchilla, orange, and Siamese.

Breeds from left to right:
1. *satin dwarf*
2. *lionhead*
3. *lionhead lop*
4. *Dalmatian rex*
5. *rex dwarf lop*

x

Rabbit Breeds | 13

Building Trust

Rabbits are great companions. If you spend a lot of time with your rabbit, she will soon become an affectionate pet.

Among Our Favorite Pets

Along with cats, dogs, and guinea pigs, rabbits are among our favorite pets. No wonder—they are soft and cuddly, cute and clean, and they can also be easily kept in a house or apartment. Rabbits can make great friends, especially for kids. They listen patiently while you talk to them, and you can have a lot of fun when you let your pet rabbit out of her cage after school. But before you take the next step, there are some things to consider and plan for so that you enjoy a great life with your new rabbit.

Rabbits Do Not Need Licenses

Unlike for a dog or cat, you do not need a license to keep a pet rabbit, but some cities may have rules about how many you can have. Check with your local government. If you rent a house or apartment, have your parents check with the landlord to make sure it is okay to have a rabbit. Also, you may need to ask your landlord if your rabbit is allowed to run around outside in the yard.

14   *Rabbits: Keeping and Caring for Your Pet*

Are You Ready for a Rabbit?

Test

Carefully consider the following questions and answer them the best you can:

☐ Do I have enough time to care for my rabbit every day, for the rest of his life? (Rabbits can live up to ten to twelve years.)

☐ Do I have enough space in my apartment for a large cage and an area of grass that my rabbit can run around on?

☐ Am I able to pay for all costs, not only for the food and bedding, but also any necessary visits to the vet?

☐ Are all my family members free from allergies to animal fur?

☐ Do I have friends or acquaintances who would be happy to look after my rabbit if I go on vacation?

Did you answer all questions with a "yes"? Great! Then you are ready for a rabbit!

Who could resist such a cute pet?

A Daily Responsibility

Once you decide you want a pet rabbit, you must keep an important fact in mind—your rabbit is not a toy, but a living, breathing animal. A rabbit needs care and attention. It is not enough to simply feed him and quickly clean out his cage. If you are the one who wanted the rabbit in the first place, you are responsible for the daily care of the rabbit, not your parents.

Younger Siblings

If your parents decide you are responsible enough to own a rabbit, be sure to teach your younger brother or sister how to behave around your pet. Show them the correct way to hold a rabbit and explain what a rabbit does and does not like so that your rabbit can feel safe around all your family members.

A Rabbit Needs a Buddy

Rabbits are very sociable animals and do not like living alone. Therefore, it is recommended that you buy at least two rabbits to keep each other company. This gives them the opportunity to play together and cuddle up to one another for warmth, until their owners return home. To find out which rabbits get along best together, see page 16.

Rabbits are very sociable and do not like to live alone, so, if you can, buy two or more.

It Takes Two to Tango

The Best Rabbit Roommates

Rabbits are very social group animals and feel at their best when they are with other rabbits. For pet rabbit fans, this means you should get two! It is not fair to keep just one lonesome rabbit. Even the most loving care from his human cannot replace the joy that comes from living together with another rabbit.

Getting Along

Keeping two or more rabbits that get along does not just depend on the two rabbits having grown up together. It depends more on the individual characters of the rabbits as to whether or not they will bond, and also whether it is a male (buck) or a female (doe), how old they are, and whether they have both been properly socialized. However, it is much easier to choose two rabbits from the same litter, as they will have known each other since birth and will have already been well socialized with each other.

Spayed Doe and Neutered Buck

The most successful combination is the spayed doe and the neutered buck. Altered rabbits are more loving and calm. They will be less likely to engage in destructive and aggressive behaviors. Also, spaying or neutering will prevent them from developing cancers in their reproductive organs. If you are new to keeping rabbits, then this combination is highly recommended.

Doe and Doe

Keeping two female rabbits is not a good idea. Females can be quite aggressive toward each other, and there may be many fights between the two of them. However, if you add a neutered buck to the combination, this will calm them down. He will settle the disputes and not get involved in any of the fights.

Buck and Buck

Despite what many people think, two bucks will tolerate each other quite well. However, they will both need to be neutered before they reach sexual maturity at about twelve weeks of age.

The best pairing is a neutered buck and a spayed doe.

16 | *Rabbits: Keeping and Caring for Your Pet*

Socializing Two or More Rabbits

If you have only one rabbit and you wish to introduce another rabbit, you should do this slowly and carefully. You cannot just stick the new rabbit in with the old rabbit. It could cause them to fight and hurt one another. You would be surprised at how aggressive your cute and cuddly little friends can become! This does not mean that your rabbit does not want company, but the sudden presence of another rabbit in his territory, even a female rabbit, is seen as a threat.

The correct way to socialize rabbits:

1. You will need a neutral space, for example, a room that neither rabbit has ever been in before.
2. Make several connecting "burrows" from cardboard boxes, with entrances and exits. Put hay, water, and food in each one.
3. Now place the two rabbits in the room at the same time. Allow them to explore the new environment. Once they have done this, the ranking order will have been established. They will probably growl at first, chase one another, and tussle a bit, which is perfectly fine, but if there is any biting, you will need to intervene and separate the animals.
4. As soon as the rabbits are eating together (and hopefully, even cuddling up to one another), then the socialization process is complete. Now you can put the two rabbits in the same enclosure, but be sure to thoroughly clean the enclosure first.

Rabbits and Guinea Pigs

Many people think it is a good idea to keep a guinea pig and a rabbit together. But this is not really ideal because the two animals have different needs, body language, and social behaviors. Often the guinea pig is the one being harassed by the rabbit. You can allow rabbits and guinea pigs to socialize as long as there are at least two of each type of animal, and they have their own cages.

If properly socialized, a group of rabbits can live happily together.

A rabbit and a guinea pig can run around and play together, but they should always be kept in separate cages.

Home Sweet Home
The Ideal Rabbit Hutch

Once you have decided on the ideal rabbit hutch for your new rabbits, you will probably be anxious to go out and buy your rabbits right away. But before you bring them home, you will need to make sure you have set up the hutch properly with the correct accessories. Then your new rabbits can settle in as soon as they arrive, and you can spend plenty of time playing with them.

Big Is Best

When you visit a pet supply store, you will see that rabbit hutches are available in every shape, size, and color. Which one would your rabbit like the best? It is simple: the biggest one! So choose the largest rabbit hutch you can find. The minimum cage size recommended by the American Society for the Prevention of Cruelty to Animals (ASPCA) is four feet long, two feet wide, and two feet high for one small- to medium-sized rabbit. Obviously if you have a giant breed, the cage will have to be larger. Also, the more animals you keep, the bigger the cage should be.

Front or Side Door

As prey animals, rabbits instinctively flee when they are frightened. Especially in the beginning, they will be very shy and easily panicked, especially if something large and dark approaches from above and swoops in to pick them up as a bird of prey would. The genetic programming of a rabbit means that his brain will scream "Predator! Run away!" even if it is just your hand going into the cage to stroke him. This is why it is better to have a cage with a door at the front or side, rather than on top, so that they can see you as you approach. They will find this less threatening than being swooped on from above.

Two Compartments

Some pet rabbit cages consist of two parts that clip onto each other: a wire cage and a deep plastic base that goes under the cage to catch the waste. This makes the cage easier to clean because you can just pull out the base, but the wire floor of the cage can hurt your rabbit's feet. If you cannot find a cage with solid flooring, you should cover the wire cage floor with a piece of wood or a sisal (a ropy material) or grass mat.

Rabbit Duplex

Rabbit cages with a second floor are a great idea. The rabbits can access this second floor by using a ramp. This is a great way to increase the rabbits' overall space and create an additional "bedroom" and add a bit of variety.

Be Creative

If you are good at do-it-yourself projects, you could even try building your own rabbit cage! You will find

Rabbits need space! Buy the biggest hutch you can find so your rabbit has plenty of room to stretch out, stand up on his hind legs, and move around.

many different designs and assembly instructions on the Internet. Some are very complex, with multiple floors, and some are even big enough to fill an entire room! Feel free to be inspired if you are feeling creative. However, do not forget the main priority: the homemade cage has to be strong and secure, not dangerous for the rabbit in any way, and also easy to clean.

Bedding

A rabbit's home must be clean and dry. Therefore, the bedding should be very good at absorbing moisture and odors. Only use natural products with no chemical additives. Do not buy straw or hay that is dusty or damp. It could irritate the breathing passages or cause feces to stick to the fur. Do not use pine or cedar shavings. The strong scents can cause breathing problems.

Wood Pulp and Pellet Litter

Pet supply stores sell wood pulp as small animal bedding; it is well suited for rabbits. Just make sure there is no cedar or pine in it. Aspen shavings are acceptable. You can also use hay or paper pellets. Although the pellets seem rather hard at first, after a short time they soften

Scatter plenty of bedding into the rabbit cage so that the ground is soft and absorbent. Rabbits like to dig into their bedding.

underfoot and become very absorbent, and the rabbit can hop around and sit on them quite comfortably. As rabbits are very clean animals, they tend to leave their droppings in one particular corner of the cage so it will be quite easy for you to clean up after them. You may want to consider training your rabbit to use a litter box. Just do not fill it with cat litter because it could make your rabbit sick.

→ *The Wrong Bedding*

It is not a good idea to use hay exclusively as bedding because the rabbit will eat it, even if it has been soiled. Also, certain materials can be harmful to your rabbit, such as newspaper, sawdust and chips, cedar and pine shavings, cat litter, and peat.

Nest Boxes, Bowls, and More

So your rabbit's new home is filled with good bedding, but it still looks empty. Here are some ideas for accessories you can put in his cage to make a hutch a home.

Nest Box

Rabbits are natural burrowers and need a safe haven. If you have two rabbits or more, you should provide each rabbit with a nest box so each animal has its own hiding place. Make sure the nest box is large enough for your rabbit and that it does not get too hot or humid inside. There are several types available, including ones made from plastic, wood, and grass. In addition, the nest box should have one entrance and one exit so that a lower-ranking animal can slip away easily if a higher-ranking rabbit pushes his way in. Windows may look nice, but rabbits could get stuck if they attempt to climb through them. A nest box with a flat roof is the best option because it gives your rabbit an opportunity to sit on top and use it as a lookout. If his nest box is damaged over time, promptly replace it to keep your pet from getting injured.

A nest box is important for a rabbit. It provides your pet with somewhere to hide and can also be used as a lookout.

Food Bowls and Hayrack

Buy two food bowls, a smaller one for dry food and a larger one for fresh food. The bowls should be sturdy and solid so they cannot be knocked over easily, and large enough for two rabbits to eat from them at the same time, if you have more than one rabbit. Generally, steel, glass, or ceramic bowls are better than plastic because they are heavier and less likely to be damaged. Tiny scratches and knicks can form in plastic and harbor bacteria.

Rabbits require hay at all times. You could either leave it loose in the cage or put it in a hayrack so that it does not get soiled. The rack can be attached to the cage, and some have a cover so your rabbit cannot climb into it.

Water Bowl or Water Bottle
Make sure your rabbit always has fresh drinking water available. You can either keep the water in a bowl or bottle.

Water Bottle
The water inside a bottle will not get dirty too quickly. However, some rabbits are unable to get enough water from the bottle, despite how hard they try. It is important to change the water daily, no matter how full the bottle may be. The bottle itself should also be thoroughly cleaned to avoid a buildup of algae, which is harmful to a rabbit's health.

Water Bowl
A water bowl—which should be solid, stable, and clean—on the cage floor is easier to drink from because the rabbit's head would be in a more natural position when he drinks. Place it on a tile so it does not get dirty too quickly, or, if possible, put it on the second floor of the cage.

→ **The Right Location**

Where should you put the rabbit cage? Find a place with plenty of light, but not somewhere that is exposed to direct sunlight or drafts. A place where there is a lot of coming and going is unsuitable, so look for somewhere a bit quieter but not hidden away in the corner. A rabbit is a sociable animal and will like to be able to see you and your family. And because domestic rabbits feel threatened by anything that comes toward them from above, it is a good idea to put the cage on a table or a dresser.

Less Is More
Besides the basic necessities, there is a huge variety of "rabbit furniture" available to decorate his cage with. You could buy a bridge, cork pipe, nest box, ramp, and other fun objects. But remember: less is more. All these things will take up space and if the cage is too full, the rabbit will not be able to stretch his legs or hop around. Put one or two items in the cage at a time, and then swap these around for a bit of variety. You could also put a couple of items in his outdoor enclosure.

Hollow cork tubes make ideal tunnels for rabbits.

Tip

Bottle or Bowl?

If you do not know your rabbit very well yet, then let him choose which he prefers. Put both a bowl and a bottle in the cage, and observe which one he uses.

Choose Wisely

Healthy House Rabbits

Perhaps you are looking for a colorful, spotted rabbit or a solid-colored rabbit with large floppy ears? No matter which type you choose, the most important thing is that he is in good health.

Where Can I Find a Rabbit?

There are several possibilities. Almost every good-sized pet shop will sell rabbits in all sorts of different colors with different types of fur. Just make sure the store is clean and the animals are well kept. You could also buy your rabbit from a breeder. Rabbit breeding is a fairly common practice, and you may even know someone whose rabbit has just had babies. And in many animal shelters or animal welfare organizations, there are plenty of cute rabbits waiting for new, loving homes. So keep your eyes open and see what you can find!

Separate Enclosures

When buying your rabbit, check that he or she has been kept in a separate cage according to gender. Otherwise you may unknowingly bring a pregnant rabbit home with you and end up with more rabbits than you bargained for. Animal welfare shelters often neuter males and spay females to prevent unwanted babies.

You can find healthy rabbits in a good pet shop, from a reputable breeder, or from an animal welfare organization.

Healthy rabbits are lively and curious. They have a dense, glossy coat and shiny eyes.

Not Too Young

Baby rabbits should be at least eight weeks old before they settle into a new home. From this age, their digestive system is able to cope with a variety of different foods, and they also will have had a chance to develop their social skills. Do not take a rabbit home if she is younger than eight weeks old because there may be a higher chance she could get ill or develop behavioral problems.

Perform a Health Check

No matter where you decide to get your rabbit from, you should give her a thorough health check before you take her home. The checklist provided will help you to distinguish between a healthy rabbit and a sick one.

Moving Into a New Home

Take your new rabbit home in a pet carrier. Cover it with a blanket to help keep her calm on the journey home. Take a direct route home, and make sure she is neither too hot nor too cold or exposed to any drafts in the car.

A Healthy Pet Rabbit Should . . .

→ have been kept in a clean, spacious enclosure, and separated according to gender. The enclosure should have somewhere for her to hide, and she should have water and hay available at all times.

→ be neither too fat nor too thin.

→ be at least eight weeks old before you take her home.

→ have clear, bright, shiny eyes with no tears. The eyes should not be swollen or have crusty mucus around them.

→ have a dry nose. Also, the mouth and ears should be dry and clean.

→ have a bite with no abnormalities. The incisors should fit well together and be worn down to equal lengths.

→ have a thick, glossy coat with no parasites. The skin underneath should be free of boils and red patches, and the rabbit should not be scratching herself.

→ have a soft stomach, not hard and bloated.

→ have a clean bottom with no feces stuck around the anus. She should not have diarrhea.

→ smell of fresh hay and clean bedding.

→ have clean soles without any scabs or crust on them.

→ be alert, awake, and curious. The tail should be sticking straight up.

→ have a healthy appetite.

→ move quickly and nimbly and not limp.

FUN TIPS

Your New Best Friend

How to Bond With Your Rabbit

So you have your new rabbit at last! Of course you will want to pick him up and show him off to all your friends, but do not forget everything is still very new to your rabbit. He will need some time to get to know you and his new home first.

Spend Time With Your Rabbit

Simply sit down in front of the cage and watch your rabbit. Do rabbits have a secret language? What does your bunny do all day? Talk to him gently in a calm, soothing voice and move slowly so you do not startle him.

Little Treats

After a few days, you will have gotten to know each other quite well, and your rabbit will not be so quick to hide when he hears you coming. It is now a good time to offer your rabbit a bunch of parsley or a carrot. Wait patiently until your rabbit's curiosity overcomes him and he comes over to see what you have. It will not take long!

Feed Him by Hand

It may take several days or even weeks, but your rabbit will soon come to recognize you as that kind person who brings him treats. Once he is eating confidently from your hand, you could try to gently scratch his head. If your rabbit tilts his head toward you and keeps it still, this is a good sign—he enjoys being stroked!

Pick Him Up

Now that you know him well enough, you can carefully pick up your rabbit. Caress his ears first, then put one hand on his neck behind his ears and your other hand under his bottom to support him. Pick him up carefully! Some rabbits may squirm quite a bit at first, so make sure you hold him firmly without hurting him, and do not let him fall!

Have Patience

It is very important to be calm and patient. Do not make any sudden movements toward your rabbit. Otherwise he may feel afraid of you. Simply lie on the floor and let him climb on you!

Friendly Greeting

Your rabbit will soon show you he is happy to see you. Some rabbits even follow their owners around everywhere and can learn amazing tricks. If you are gentle and kind to your rabbit, then he will soon become your best friend.

What Your Rabbit Needs

Living Space

Rabbits like to live in a large cage filled with a thick layer of fresh bedding. The best type of cage should have a solid floor so your rabbit does not hurt her feet. There should be room for her to dig and run around. The entrance should be on the side of the cage and have a small ramp leading up to the cage so your rabbit can climb in and out.

Sleeping Area

You should provide each of your rabbits with his or her own nest box with one entrance and one exit. Rabbits like dark, cozy spaces where they feel safe and have somewhere to hide. The nest box should be big enough for your rabbit to stretch out comfortably. The best type of nest box is one with a flat roof so your rabbit can sit on top and keep an eye on her surroundings.

Shopping List

→ pet carrier
→ large cage
→ bedding
→ nest box
→ food
→ water bowl or bottle
→ hayrack
→ litter box
→ rabbit furniture, such as a cork tube

→ treats (fresh hay, fruit, and vegetables, perhaps some dry food)

Other items:

→ safety measures for the balcony
→ an outdoor enclosure to run around in

Eating

Rabbits are always hungry, but they do not have the best table manners. Your rabbit will need two sturdy food bowls and a water bowl or bottle. Sometimes rabbits hop in and out of their food bowls, so make sure they are solid and stable. It is best to put the hay in a hayrack, otherwise she will hop around, sleep, dig, and go to the bathroom in it.

Litter Box

Rabbits are very clean and tend to leave their droppings in the same place each time. Therefore, a rabbit can be housebroken quite easily, and you can provide her with a litter box to use when you let her run around in the house or yard.

Playing

Not all rabbits like to play ball games, but almost all of them love to investigate tunnels and tubes. How about giving her a cork tube or a clay pipe? Also, bridges or large branches are great objects to climb around on, but do not make her enclosure so full that she has no room to hop around.

Safe Transportation

Buy a pet carrier for your rabbit. It is well worth it because not only will you need it to bring her home, but also to take her to the vet from time to time. The carrier will keep her safe and she will not be able to nibble her way out of it.

Grooming

Rabbits spend quite a lot of time grooming themselves. Short-haired breeds do not need too much help, but long-haired breeds will need to be groomed regularly to stop their fur from becoming tangled and matted.

Caring for Your Rabbit

The Way to the Heart Is Through the Stomach
Healthy Food for Rabbits

What Is a Rabbit's Favorite Activity?

Eating, of course! To make sure your little friend eats well, here is a brief insight into what to feed your rabbit.

Rabbits may eat up to eighty small meals a day, mostly consisting of hay. Rabbits need hay to help with digestion and also to wear their teeth down.

A Varied Diet

Wild rabbits feast on a variety of different foods; they love to nibble on any form of fresh greens, as well as dried grasses or leaves, buds, bark and branches, roots, and seeds. They also make the most of nature's very own pharmacy and eat herbs that contain natural defenses to strengthen their immune system. Our pet rabbits are not any different and prefer a varied diet as well, so make sure you provide plenty of variety.

Plenty of Food

Rabbits have to eat constantly in order to maintain good health and keep their strength up. Over the course of a day, a rabbit may eat up to eighty meals! This is not because they are greedy. Rabbits have a very long colon, so their food is not moved along the colon as quickly as in the case of humans. Their digestive system needs a steady food supply to keep the intestinal contents moving along the colon. In other words, every time food is digested, the food that is already in the colon moves a little farther along. This is why you need to ensure that your rabbit has a constant food supply available—especially hay—so that he can eat whenever he needs to. If a rabbit has been deprived of food for a sustained period and is then given a large quantity of food, he will eat too quickly and too much at once, rather than little and often as his digestive system requires. The result is that the contents of his intestine will not move along the colon; rather, the food ferments and rots in the gut, causing gas and very painful indigestion. This is why eating little and often is very important for a rabbit.

Double Digestion

You may have already noticed that your rabbit eats his own feces. Although we might think this is disgusting, do not stop him from doing it because it is actually vital for his digestion.

Rabbits love to nibble on branches, and this is also a great way to wear down their teeth.

Recycling the Rabbit Way

Rabbits do not just eat any old feces though—they carefully select the moist, greenish brown round pellets called cecotropes. Cecotropes are actually partially digested food formed in the cecum, a pouch located where the small intestine and the large intestine meet, which is the same place a human appendix would be. In the cecum, good bacteria breaks down food that is too hard to digest the first time around, producing nutrient-rich cecotropes. It is from these cecotropes that a rabbit gets the majority of his nutrition, not from the first passage of food through the gut. This ensures he gets as many nutrients as possible from indigestible plant food, such as protein and vitamins (mainly vitamin B). It also cleanses the inside of the colon.

Eating Helps With Dental Hygiene

Rabbits' teeth grow constantly, at about the same pace as our fingernails. A rabbit's teeth grow one to two millimeters per week, which ensures they do not wear down completely as they get older.

The longer a rabbit spends biting, chewing, and grinding up his food, the better. It is not so much the hardness of the food that is important, but more so the fact that his teeth are constantly being ground together.

Rabbits nibble constantly. Hay is the best food for your rabbit.

Eating Is a Pastime

Of course, food also keeps a rabbit busy. So that your rabbit does not become overweight, you should provide him with the right food: plenty of hay as well as fruit and vegetables. And remember, the best exercise for him is being able to run around with his rabbit buddies in the house or yard.

Delicious Every Day

Hay, Water, Straw, and Branches

Rabbits love to munch on hay or even just relax in it.

As you now know, your rabbit needs to eat constantly. But the food must be right for her! Her staple foods are hay and water, as well as herbs, fruit, and vegetables.

Hay Morning, Noon, and Night

Hay is the most important food for your pet rabbit. It is high in fiber, contains minerals and trace elements, and also helps to wear down the teeth. It can be eaten in unlimited quantities. It is best to replace the hay three times a day. Either put it in a hayrack or spread it around the cage. The quality of the hay depends on how many types

How to Spot Good Quality Hay

→ It should contain visible herbs, many different types of grasses with leaves, flowers, and buds.

→ The stems should be about eight to fourteen inches long.

→ Good quality hay is green, not gray.

→ It should smell aromatic, not musty.

→ Hay should be grown in organic meadows and not polluted by pesticides.

→ Hay must be kept dry, and dust- and mold-free.

of wild herbs are found within it, as well as the mineral content of the soil in which it was grown, when it was mowed, and how it was dried and stored. Bad hay is gray in color, musty smelling, sticky, dusty, and moldy. It is harmful to your rabbit and could give him bad indigestion.

What About Straw?

Straw is normally used as bedding rather than food. Nevertheless, rabbits do like to nibble on it. Straw is not as rich in nutrients as hay, but very high in fiber. Chewing on straw wears down the teeth and keeps a rabbit busy. Because straw fields are much more frequently treated with pesticides and fertilizer than hay fields, it often contains more harmful residues than hay. So do not give your rabbit too much straw, or buy straw that has been grown organically.

Water, the Elixir of Life

It may not appear to you that your rabbit drinks very much water. But she will drink a fair amount, especially if she only has access to hay and dry food. Make sure she always has fresh water in her cage and when she is outside in her exercise pen. Do not give your rabbit milk to drink. It contains lactose, which may lead to digestive disorders, such as diarrhea. Also be aware that distilled water is harmful to rabbits.

Fresh Branches

Fresh branches are also an important part of your rabbit's diet. Branches serve two purposes: they entertain her and contain valuable nutrients. Your rabbit will love to nibble on the leaves or buds, peel the bark, and shred the wood. Branches wear down their teeth and contain vegetable

oils as well. Ideal branches include those from fruit trees (apple and pear), hazelnut, beeches, poplars, alders, and willows, as long as they have not been sprayed with fertilizer.

Fresh branches are good for your rabbit and will keep her busy. You could hide a combination of branches and hay in various places inside her cage.

Lion's Share of Roughage   Tip

Hay, straw, and branches are what is known as roughage. Eighty percent of a rabbit's diet is roughage, which is mainly provided by hay.

Bring on the Vegetables!

Vitamin-Rich Greens

You can grow your own vegetables and grasses and surprise your rabbit with a few fresh treats, even in wintertime!

Soft foods such as vegetables and grasses aid digestion and provide essential nutrients.

Greens, Greens, and More Greens

Herbs and vegetables contain numerous vitamins and minerals. The ASPCA recommends a minimum of two cups of fresh leafy greens per six pounds of body weight per day. If your rabbit is used to eating grass, then she may be able to tolerate more than this.

Gather Weeds and Herbs

Perfect for rabbits, weeds grow almost anywhere. It is best to pick them from uncultivated meadows or lawns and gardens, where there is an abundant growth of plants. Plants from lawns and gardens that have been treated, roads and roadsides, railway embankments, areas where people walk their dogs, and sprayed and fertilized fields should be left alone. Pick clean, dry plants and give your rabbit as much as she can eat every day. Store the plants in an airy container and keep them somewhere cool. Throw away any uneaten weeds or herbs after about half a day.

Homegrown Greens

Homegrown greens from your windowsill will definitely be gratefully received by your rabbit. If you happen to have a green thumb, you could grow these from seed mixes or grow fast-germinating plant species, such as grass, clover, and sow grain. Keep the soil moist and after about three weeks of growth, you can treat your pet. Just make sure mold has not formed on the plant. Never feed anything that has become moldy, stale, wilted, or rotten to your rabbit.

If you do not want to grow your own vegetables, then you could buy a cat grass pot plant, which you can find in any pet supply store or garden center. You can also buy trays of herbs as well.

→ Your Rabbit's Favorite Foods

Herbs

alfalfa
balm
bishop's weed
chamomile
comfrey
dandelion
dill
grasses with panicles
(clusters at the end of
a shoot)
lovage
marigold
mugwort
nettle leaves
parsley
peppermint
plantain
sage
yarrow

Vegetables

broccoli
carrots with or without
leaves
celery
chicory
cucumber (very small
amount)
endive (small amount)
fennel
Jerusalem artichoke
kohlrabi leaves
pepper
rutabaga

Get Crunching: Delicious Vegetables

Rabbits love fresh, crisp vegetables. Wash and dry them before putting them in the cage. You could hide the vegetables in the hayrack or poke them into the bars of the cage for a bit of variety. Again, make sure you clear away any uneaten fresh food after half a day because it will soon begin to wilt.

What does your rabbit like the best? Offer her different vegetables and watch to see which ones she eats first.

A Change in Diet   Tip

Introduce a change in diet slowly and gradually. Only offer small amounts of the new food at first and then increase the amount slowly over a few days. This also applies to new grass after the winter is over. Provide your rabbit with hay first and foremost and then a small amount of grass.

Sweet Treats
Fruit for Healthy Rabbits

The mainstay of a rabbit's diet is hay, grass, herbs, and crunchy vegetables. However, as a special treat you can give your rabbit a small amount of fresh fruit.

An Apple a Day . . .

. . . Keeps the doctor away. Or rather the vet because this saying also applies to rabbits. Apples aid a rabbit's digestion and prevent intestinal problems. Give your rabbit a piece of apple every day, without the core. Other fruits, such as melon, will be gratefully received, but only give your rabbit small quantities every now and again because most fruits contain a lot of sugar.

Vitamin C

Rose hips, fresh or dried, contain a lot of vitamin C. Your rabbit will greatly appreciate these!

Tasty Fruit for Special Occasions

As already mentioned, most fruits contain sugar but you can give your rabbit some fruit every two to three days. Rabbits love pears (without the core), blackberries, or melon. Some rabbits are also crazy about bananas, but these are very high in sugar and can lead to constipation.

Fruit enriches a rabbit's diet. Apple is particularly good because it is easily digested by a rabbit.

Tips on Feeding Your Rabbit

→ Clean out the bowls daily.

→ Fresh hay and clean water should always be available.

→ Make the food as varied and interesting as possible.

→ Introduce any new type of food slowly and in small amounts.

→ Make sure fruits, vegetables, and fresh greens are freshly washed and then dried. Remove the core from apples and other fruit. Remove any uneaten food from the cage after half a day.

→ Do not give her cold food straight from the refrigerator.

→ Avoid feeding your rabbit cabbage (causes bloating), lettuce (often overfertilized), stale bread, and yogurt. Yogurt contains milk and rabbits should not consume dairy products because they have lactose and your rabbit cannot digest this.

Share With Your Rabbit

Share your fruit with your rabbit. You could give her small amounts of the fruit you eat. Raspberry and blackberry leaves, blueberry stalks and leaves, and strawberry leaves are all favorites with rabbits.

Dry Food

If your pet rabbit has a balanced diet, as described above, she will not actually need any dry food. Fresh hay, fruit, vegetables, herbs, and branches will provide her with all the nutrients she needs. If you want to feed her a small amount of dry food, however, go for a mix that does not contains grains, for example, alfalfa pellets, or dry food made from clover and other herbs.

When and How Much?

You could give your rabbit some dry food for her breakfast, but only once she has finished her hay. The hay will stimulate the digestive system and wear down the teeth. Each rabbit should get no more than one-eighth to one-quarter of a cup of dry food per five pounds of body weight per day. Your rabbit may eat her dry food first and then get full and not eat her hay. So make sure she gets her hay first!

A rabbit does not actually need dry food, but if you wish to feed it to her then make sure she eats her hay first.

FUN TIPS

Snack Ideas for Rabbits

Everyone enjoys fun, tasty snacks! Even rabbits!

Obviously, snacks for a rabbit do not include potato chips or chocolate bars, but you will see how much your rabbit will enjoy the following snack ideas, and you could even try them yourself!

Colorful Kebab

Find a long, thick piece of straw. Slice up a variety of fruit and vegetables, such as carrot, cucumber, bell pepper, and apple. String the straw through the pieces of food in rainbow order. You can hang these kebabs from the top of the cage as a sort of edible decoration.

Veggies on a Brick

For this snack idea, you will need a brick. Chop up different-colored vegetables, such as carrots, fennel, or red pepper, into pieces small enough to push into the holes in the brick. Then your rabbit has to put in a bit of effort to get her food out of the holes.

Dangling Apple

Use a corer to remove the core from an apple. Now thread a piece of string through the empty core and dangle it in front of your rabbit. If you hold the apple just out of reach, your rabbit will have to stand up and "dance" on her hind legs to reach it, which is a great workout!

Food Bells

Food bells are easy to make and look great, too! All you need are some miniature flowerpots, fresh vegetables, and a piece of string. Tie a piece of carrot, for example, to the string, then thread the other end of the string through the hole in the flowerpot and tie it to the roof of the cage.

Some Rules for the Best Bunny Owners!

Your rabbit likes
→ very quiet music
→ fresh, crunchy snacks
→ cuddling without being forced

Your rabbit does not like
→ loud music and crowds
→ old, moldy, or wilted food
→ being picked up and forced to have a cuddle

Well-Groomed Rabbits

Rabbits are very neat and clean animals. They groom themselves extensively and also groom their rabbit buddies. This means you will not have to groom her too much—every now and then will be enough.

Grooming

You do not really need to brush your rabbit, unless she has long fur. However, some rabbits do enjoy being gently groomed with a grooming mitt. She may also appreciate a back scratch for all those hard-to-reach places. Grooming your rabbit serves three purposes at once: it strengthens the bond between you and your rabbit, it removes any loose fur (especially during shedding season), and it allows you to examine the fur for parasites (fleas, mites, or lice).

Rabbits place a lot of importance on personal hygiene. They lick, nibble, and rub their fur until they are clean from head to toe.

→ Please Do Not Bathe Your Rabbit!

Rabbits do not need or like baths, and they certainly do not need shampoo. They are very clean animals by nature, so giving your rabbit a bath is not necessary. If she has a spell of diarrhea and could use a wash, clean her bottom with a damp cloth and warm water and dry her off with a towel.

Health Check

If your rabbit is ill, you may not realize it until it is too late. Rabbits do not like to show they are sick or they will be left by their group and therefore become easy prey for predators. So it is a good idea to perform a quick health check while you are cuddling your rabbit so that you may catch any early signs of disease or other health problems.

From Head to Toe

Is your rabbit eating well? Is she eating as much as she usually does, at her usual speed? Is she alert and interested in her surroundings? Is she hopping around as normal? Are her eyes clear? Is her nose dry? Are her ears clean? Hold up the ears and have a look inside the ear canal. Does her belly feel soft? Are her feet clean and free from injuries? Take a look at her bottom; check the genitals and anus and make sure they are clean with no mucus. If there is any mucus on these areas, you can clean this away with a damp cloth. The better you know your rabbit, the sooner you will recognize changes in her and catch any problems early on.

Show Me Your Feet

Rabbits have five claws on each front paw and four claws on each back paw. In the wild, they use their front paws as digging tools, which wears the claws down, and they grow back quickly. Your rabbit probably will not have many opportunities to dig as she would in the wild, so you will need to trim her claws regularly.

Pedicure

Trim your rabbit's claws using a special clipper that can be bought from any good pet supply store. This is a job for two

→ Weight Control

Weigh your rabbit once a week. The best way to do this is to put her in a bowl attached to a set of scales so she cannot run away, and this will ensure the reading is more accurate. Make a weight card for each rabbit and record his or her weight each week on the card. This way, you will be able to see at a glance whether your pet's weight has suddenly gone up or down.

people ideally; one of you can hold the rabbit while the other cuts her claws. Do this in front of a good source of light so you can see where the blood vessels and nerves are in the claws. Cut about three to five millimeters from the tips horizontally. If she has very dark claws and you cannot see the blood vessels, then only cut a tiny amount to be on the safe side, and do this more often. Get your vet to show you how to cut your rabbit's claws the first time.

Say "Ahh!"

If a rabbit's teeth are not worn down enough, this will make it difficult for her to eat. Your vet will be able to tell you whether this has been caused by a poor diet or an abnormality. The vet will be able to trim her teeth for her. Dwarf rabbits often have dental problems because their jaws are too narrow.

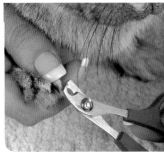

If the claws are too long, use a special clipper to trim them.

Clear eyes? Neat claws? Clean ears? A rabbit health check does not need to take too long.

Taking Your Rabbit to the Vet

A large cage, lots of space to run around, loving care, fresh hay, water, fruit, and vegetables are essential to keeping your rabbit healthy. But even if you do everything right, your rabbit may still get sick. If you suspect your rabbit may be ill, take her to the vet without delay.

If you notice something is wrong with your rabbit, then you should act immediately. The quicker the problem is caught, the better her chances are of recovering.

Vaccinations for Rabbits

There are no approved vaccinations for pet rabbits in the United States. Other countries, for example England and Australia, do vaccinate their rabbits against certain diseases. If your rabbit becomes ill, the only thing you can do is take her to the vet for treatment.

Caring for your rabbit and feeding her a healthy diet is the best disease prevention there is.

Better to Be Safe Than Sorry

It is best to take your rabbit to the vet as soon as possible if you suspect something is wrong. It may take the vet a while to work out what the problem is before treatment can begin, so do not delay.

Choosing a Vet

Not all vets specialize in the treatment of small animals. Some specialize in cats, dogs, or horses. Look for a vet experienced in treating rabbits as soon as you can. Do not wait for a medical emergency to find out where to take your rabbit. Have the vet's number and address some place you can easily access them.

Questions the Veterinarian May Ask

Transport your rabbit in her pet carrier, and do not forget her weight log card. If you suspect that your pet rabbit has eaten something poisonous, then bring a sample of this poison with you to the veterinarian's office. Your vet will ask you for information about your rabbit. The more precisely you can answer your vet's questions, the better. Here are some examples of what the vet may ask you:

→ How old is the animal?
→ How long have you had her?
→ Where and how is she kept?
→ When did you first notice any symptoms?
→ What has changed?
→ Does she have an appetite and thirst?
→ What has she eaten and drunk?
→ Are her feces normal?
→ Has she made any sounds or engaged in certain behaviors that may indicate she is in pain?

Stress-Free Visit to the Vet

Rabbits do not particularly enjoy going to the vet. To make it a bit nicer for her, bring one of her rabbit buddies along for the journey. The presence of her pal will reassure her. Put a towel on the bottom of her carrier as well as some fresh hay and a carrot to nibble on to distract her from her anxieties.

Make a List

Make a list of questions before you go so that you do not forget to ask something in all the rush. When the vet has made the diagnosis, ask him to clearly explain everything to you. Ask him if you should schedule another appointment, and also make sure you are clear on the dosage instructions of any prescribed medication. Should your rabbit be kept separately from her buddies or is she okay to remain in her cage? Also, have the vet show you how to give your pet the medicine.

When Rabbits Age

All pet rabbits will grow old eventually. Sometimes you will notice significant signs of aging by the sixth or seventh year, although some rabbits will age later than this.

Aging

Older rabbits will not be inclined to move about as much or climb as easily as they did when they were younger. Provide her with a small ramp to climb in and out of her cage, and also make sure she can reach her water and food bowls easily. An older animal will not want to move around as much, so make sure you give her lots of cuddles instead.

Farewell

Usually when rabbits die, they pass away in their sleep without suffering. Try to take some comfort from the fact that this is a natural part of life, and your rabbit is not scared of dying. You gave her a lifetime of love and kindness, and you will always have the great memories.

Weigh your rabbit regularly to keep an eye on her weight. Then you will be able to tell if she has suddenly put on weight or lost it.

Older rabbits want peace and quiet. They will probably not be as eager to hop about and will prefer to snuggle up with you instead.

→ *The Most Common Rabbit Illnesses*

Symptoms	Suspected Cause	Treatment
diarrhea, mushy droppings, or watery diarrhea	a sudden change in diet, malocclusion (teeth are not aligned correctly), bacterial infection, intestinal parasites, poisoning	Feed him hay and water only. No watery foods. If the diarrhea has not subsided after twenty-four hours, take him to the vet. If he has watery diarrhea, take him to the vet immediately, and take a feces sample with you.
ruffled fur, heavy breathing, a hard and firm belly, and stamping on the ground with hind legs	bloat	Immediately remove all food except hay and water and go to the vet as soon as possible.
large droppings or none at all	constipation, hairball caused by excess shedding, too little exercise	Brush your rabbit whenever he sheds. Allow sufficient movement. Put a drop of rapeseed oil on a slice of pineapple or kiwi to help speed up his digestion and get rid of the hairball. If constipation continues, take him to the vet.
listlessness, lying on his side, refusing to eat, and shallow breathing	heat stroke, severe disease/infection	With a suspected heatstroke, take immediate action. Wrap the rabbit in a cool, damp towel, splash him with water, and also place his feet in cool water. Take him immediately to the vet. If you suspect any type of infection, go straight to the vet.

Symptoms	Suspected Cause	Treatment
red, swollen, dull eyes; red, swollen eyelids	conjunctivitis (pink eye), eye injury, cheek or tooth problems	Go to the vet.
sticky or moist nose, sneezing, loss of appetite, heavy breathing	cold virus (anything from the sniffles to pneumonia)	Avoid drafts and the cold. Keep an eye on his breathing. Take him to the vet as soon as possible.
drooling, very wet mouth, and difficulty eating	teeth problems or poor diet	Check the incisors—are they too long or is one broken? Check the back teeth as well. Get your vet to take a look.
sticky or flaky ears, tilting his head to one side	inner ear infection, parasites, or fungus	Go to the vet. The lop rabbit often has problems with clogged ears and these will need to be cleaned by the vet. In the case of parasites or fungal infection, the vet will have to do a swab test to make the correct diagnosis before he or she can prescribe medication.
dull, scruffy coat; bald patches; scabs; itching	parasite infestation (fleas, lice, mites) or fungus	Your vet will be able to diagnose this and prescribe the correct medication.
There is blood in the urine, and the rabbit finds it painful to urinate.	bladder or kidney infection	Go to the vet. He will diagnose whether it is a bladder infection, bladder stones, or kidney stones, and he will prescribe the appropriate treatment.
sore hind legs, bald patches, or scabs	inflammation caused by flooring, e.g. carpets, hard bedding, etc.	Make sure the bedding is nice and soft. Replace any bedding that is too hard. Only allow him to run around on cotton rugs. Synthetic carpets are bad for the paws—the rabbit could get carpet burns while running around.

One, Two, Three, Four, and Even More
Breeding Like Rabbits

If the doe is in heat, the buck will attempt to mate with her.

Rabbits are able to reproduce in great numbers! This is useful in the wild because a large number of rabbits are eaten by predators or die of diseases, but there are more than enough domestic rabbits in captivity. Animal shelters and animal protection organizations do not quite know what to do with them all. This is the reason it is advised that you not breed your rabbits, tempting though it may be.

Baby rabbits are incredibly cute, but it is best to leave breeding to a professional breeder.

Suddenly There They Were

It happens quite frequently. You are a proud owner of two beautiful rabbits. They live in a lovely cage and both "bucks" get along splendidly. Then, after a few weeks, you find a baby rabbit in the cage! You may have bought a pregnant female without realizing because the rabbits had not been properly sexed or kept separately. In order to prevent these sorts of surprises, you should have the vet examine your new pets to check that Ralph the rabbit is not really Rachel the rabbit.

Doe or Buck?

To identify your rabbit's sex, put him on your lap and gently turn him onto his back with his hind legs facing you.

The doe's genitals are U-shaped.

And the buck's genitals resemble a small tube.

With one hand holding the front legs high, look at the genitals. Be gentle with the fur around the genitals. Use your index and middle finger to carefully push out the genitals. A buck's genitals resemble a round tube, whereas a doe's genitals are U-shaped and directly link to the anus. It is not always easy to tell the sex if the rabbit is very young and has not reached sexual maturity. If you are unsure, ask a friend who is experienced with rabbits or check with your vet.

Altering or Sterilization

These terms are often used to mean the same thing, but there is a significant difference. Altering refers to neutering for a male and spaying for a female. When a buck is neutered, his testicles are removed. When a doe is spayed, her ovaries and uterus are taken out. In the case of sterilization, the tube that produces semen or eggs is cut. Although the animal can no longer reproduce, it still has sex hormones and all the associated problems, such as destructive behavior, aggression, or cancers of the reproductive system.

The Right Age

Depending on your rabbit's breed and gender, she or he may reach sexual maturity between three and eight months of age. So that they can live peacefully with their rabbit buddies, early altering

→ Benefits of Neutering/Spaying

Altered rabbits
- → have no offspring
- → get along better with other rabbits
- → are calmer
- → are healthier
- → mark their territory less

Eating Before Surgery **Tip**

Rabbits have very sensitive digestive systems, which means they need to eat constantly, so do not starve your rabbit before his operation. Just give him lighter foods such as hay, fennel, and carrots. Unlike dogs, cats, and humans, rabbits do not have a vomiting reflex, so rabbits are not in danger of choking on their own vomit while under anesthesia.

is recommended. The bucks can be neutered as soon as the testicles have descended into the scrotum, which is in the third month of life. Female rabbits should be spayed between heat cycles. This operation is a little more complicated, so make sure you see a veterinarian who has had experience in altering rabbits.

My Care Plan

Daily

Water

Change the water twice a day, and clean out the water bowl or bottle to prevent a buildup of bacteria.

Food

Give your rabbit fresh hay three times a day. Also, a piece of apple, carrot, or fennel and some fresh greens (dandelion leaves, grass, parsley) will complete the menu. Do not forget to remove any uneaten fresh food after half a day.

Bathroom

Rabbits are very neat and usually leave their droppings in the same corner of their cage. Clear away the droppings and soiled bedding and add fresh bedding. You may also want to train your rabbit to use a litter box. But remember, cat litter is bad for rabbits!

Exercise

Your rabbit should be let out of his cage at least once a day for a couple of hours. Make sure you keep an eye on him though.

Health Check

Healthy appetite? Shiny eyes? Dry nose? Clean bottom? Check daily that the fur is glossy, the eyes are shiny, the ears are clean, and the bottom is dry without any discharge or mucus. In short, is your rabbit healthy, frisky, and playful?

Clean Out the Cage

Once or twice a week, you will need to clean out the cage thoroughly. Remove all the bedding and scrub the base of the cage with hot water and a mild detergent. Once it has been dried, fill it with fresh bedding.

New Branches

Lots of new twigs and branches in the cage will be greatly appreciated! Give him branches from apple, pear, hazelnut, beech, poplar, or alder trees so your rabbit can chew and nibble to his heart's content.

Health Check

Take a closer look at your rabbit on a weekly basis. What about the teeth? Do they fit together nicely and have they been worn down enough? What about the claws? Do they need trimming? Also examine the ears and the soles of the feet, wipe his genital area with a damp cloth, and brush his fur.

The Big Clean

Once or twice a month, clean all the rabbit furniture from the cage by scrubbing it with hot water and mild detergent. If your rabbit has his own litter box, then you should clean this out, too. However, bear in mind that your rabbits will not like having their cage smell all nice and clean because it will not smell like them!

Vacation

If you want to go on vacation, you will have to find yourself a rabbit sitter. The best person would be someone who knows about rabbits and what they need. Ideally, your rabbit sitter should go and visit your rabbits on a daily basis to care for them. This way, they can stay in their own home and do not need to be moved. If this is not possible, then you will need to gather everything your rabbits need and take them to your friend's house.

Rabbit Boarding House

If you cannot find anyone to look after your rabbit, you will need to find a rabbit boarding house. Animal shelters, vets, and rabbit organizations, such as your local chapter of the House Rabbit Society, should be able to recommend a suitable place where your rabbits will be well cared for. Rabbits do not enjoy traveling, so it is best to get them looked after instead of taking them away with you.

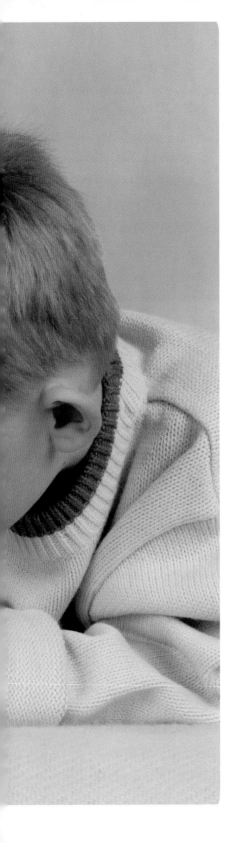

3

Understanding and Entertaining Your Rabbit

Alert and Nimble
Typical Rabbit Behavior

The more you know about your pet, the better you will understand him and the more fun the two of you can have together. So keep your eyes and ears open and your nose twitching! What are your pets trying to tell you?

Rabbits are not the bravest animals in the world. They are always ready to run away at a moment's notice. This is why they are known as flight animals.

Although rabbits have an almost 360-degree view of their surroundings, they cannot really see what is in front of their noses.

Prey Animals

Rabbits are small animals and are neither strong nor courageous. So what do they do when they sense danger? You guessed it—they run for their lives! Rabbits are flight animals, and whenever they feel threatened, they quickly disappear into hiding. And not only do they feel threatened by their natural enemies but also by loud, sudden, unfamiliar noises; new smells; and a huge human hand swooping down on them from above.

Eye Contact

Rabbits are especially fearful about anything that swoops down on them from above, such as eagles. So when you want to play with your rabbit, it is best to approach him at eye level. Play with him when you are both sitting on the floor, and also keep his cage somewhere up high. Your rabbit will take a while to adjust to anything new, such as his new cage, strange sounds, new people, and perhaps other pets. But once he has adjusted to all this, he should be very tame and trusting with you.

Panoramic View

Rabbits have movement vision and can perceive movements all around them. Because they have eyes at the sides of their heads, they have an almost 360-degree view without having to turn their heads.

However, they cannot see as well close up or see things that are happening right under their nose. They do not like bright lights and cannot differentiate between red and green. But they can see very well in low light, for example at dusk.

Super Nose

Rabbit noses are constantly moving. When a rabbit twitches his nose, more than 100 million olfactory cells are in action. Rabbits have a very good sense of smell, and they use their noses to investigate their surroundings and find out information: Where is the food? Where are my buddies? How are you today? Where are my enemies hiding? Odors such as smoke or cleaning products are very strong for a rabbit.

Scent Language

Rabbits communicate through scent. Family members and strangers are distinguished from each other, and rabbits scent mark objects or other animals using scent glands in their chin. Females attract males with special chemicals called pheromones, and a buck will scent his chosen female with his urine.

Eavesdropping

With his highly sensitive ears, a rabbit does not miss much, least of all the soft rustle of a bag of food. His ears can move back and forth independently of one another. Bear in mind that most sounds are very loud for your rabbit, and extremely loud or high frequency sounds (such as sounds made on the TV) are uncomfortable for him and will make him fearful. But a rabbit's ears are not just for listening; when it is very hot, a lot of heat is released from the ears. Rabbits cannot sweat.

Gourmet

You will soon discover rabbits are true gourmets, with very special likes and dislikes. Some foods they love while others they may reject in disgust. Unfortunately, rabbits also eat things they should not eat. That is why it is important to keep certain objects out of his reach!

Whiskers

It is not just cats that have whiskers. Rabbits also have sensitive whiskers on the right and left of the nose, the mouth, and over the eyes. These whiskers allow a rabbit to feel out his surroundings in the dark. These are important for life in a burrow so that he can move quickly through the tunnels. Do not ever trim these whiskers or pluck them!

Have you ever seen your rabbit twitch his nose? A rabbit's nose is constantly on the move! A rabbit twitches his nose to pick up all the scent messages in his surroundings.

Rabbit ears can move independently from each other and be rotated in different directions. So your rabbit will be able to hear everything, including the rustle of the food bag!

Rabbit speak

→ You will rarely hear your rabbit vocalize sounds, but from time to time rabbits make the occasional noise. If something has annoyed them they grumble to themselves.

→ A hiss or growl is used to display aggression.

→ When the buck is wooing a doe, he growls, and when mating is successfully completed, the male grunts and falls on his side.

→ When rabbits are in pain, they grind their teeth. If you hear the gnashing of teeth, you should examine your rabbit and take him to the vet.

→ Rabbits can also scream. But they do so only when they fear for their lives.

→ Sometimes rabbits whimper softly if they are picked up too quickly. If this is the case, you should put him back down again.

→ If a rabbit feels especially playful, he rolls around.

→ Another sign of physical well-being is when a rabbit stretches out on his side and murmurs to himself.

→ "I love you" in rabbit language is expressed by licking. Rabbits lick each other on the head, neck, and behind the ears.

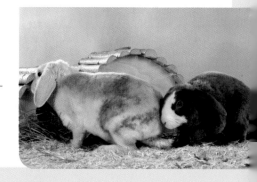

→ A slight nudge with the nose means "Hello" or "Pet me." Once he has had enough, he will push you away!

→ If a rabbit wants to inspect something, he will stand up on his hind legs to get a better look.

→ When a rabbit approaches something cautiously, he slowly hobbles toward the object with his head pushed forward, his body elongated, and his tail sticking up.

→ When in danger, they warn their fellow rabbits. And what could be a better warning signal than a drum? To do this, he pulls his hind legs under his body and beats the ground hard.

→ When a rabbit wants to threaten another rabbit, he crouches down, sticks out his bottom, and flattens his ears back. This means "Stay right where you are or I will fight you!"

Bunny Love
A Rabbit's Friendships

By now, you will have learned that rabbits do not like to be alone. They feel most at ease with at least one other rabbit, and even better when in a small group. They also like to have contact with their humans and can form good friendships with other animals. But before you attempt to mix your pets, you will need to follow certain rules to avoid any conflicts.

Rabbits can learn to get along with other animals but only really communicate effectively with other rabbits.

Birds of a Feather Flock Together

Naturally, rabbits prefer to live in the company of other rabbits. It is easy for two rabbits to get to know one another, but what happens when you want your rabbit to meet your other pets? Because rabbits communicate heavily using scents, this meeting will go better if the two animals smell like each other. Stroke one pet and then the other to mingle the two scents.

The best way to let them mix is on neutral ground so they do not fight over territory. Read more about this on page 17.

Encounters Between Rabbits and Guinea Pigs

It is a good idea to mingle the two scents. The two animals will probably get along quite well in a large space but should be kept in separate cages and live with their own kind.

Rabbits and Other Animals

Completely different animals can become good friends. Before the animals meet, you should mix their scents. Do this by stroking your rabbit, then allowing your dog to sniff your hand, and vice versa.

First Meeting

The next step is getting the animals to meet for the first time. First, keep your rabbit in his cage and allow your dog or cat to carefully smell the cage.

Make sure both animals remain calm. After the mutual curiosity has been satisfied, extensively praise all participants, and reward them with treats. This creates a positive experience for both animals. Only when the animals seem fully relaxed with each other can you let the rabbit out of his cage in the presence of your dog or cat.

→ *Do Not Let Them Out of Your Sight!*

No matter how well your rabbit and your dog or cat seem to get along, never leave them alone together unattended. Dogs and cats are predators with a natural prey drive, and their hunting instinct could suddenly take over. The friendship could be forgotten in an instant, and your rabbit could be chased or even bitten.

Your dog and rabbit could become the best of friends, but never leave them alone together.

Exercise Indoors and Outside

Even if your rabbits have a large cage, space is still fairly limited for them. Therefore, you should allow your rabbits out of their cages for at least two hours a day.

Playpen

Many rabbit owners have a playpen the rabbit can run around in as she pleases. You can buy one at a pet supply store or make one yourself. One idea is to nail

Support for the Feet

To help stop your rabbits from sliding around the floor, put some cotton rugs down. Set up the playpen with a nest box, toilet area, water, and hay. You can also provide tunnels and toys.

Exercise

Even if you do not have much space in your home, you should try to let your rabbit run around as much as possible so

Rabbits are very curious and want to explore everything. Create a whole new world of experiences for your pets! Make sure you remove any dangerous objects before your rabbits go exploring.

four wooden planks together, making sure they are high enough so the rabbit cannot climb out. There are also playpen covers you can buy to protect your rabbit from the sun if you bring her outside. You could also use the cover as flooring to protect your carpet or discourage digging. If you want to create your own flooring for the playpen, it should be linoleum or laminate so it can be easily cleaned with a mild detergent and hot water.

she can indulge her need to move around. A rabbit needs exercise to remain healthy and prevent lethargy and obesity. Your rabbit also needs variety and new sensory experiences for her well-being.

Beware of Chewing

Before you let your rabbit out, make sure you put away any objects she could chew on because rabbits like to test out their surroundings by nibbling and chewing.

This is especially important for expensive or dangerous items. Put away any cell phone, laptop, or music player chargers and poisonous houseplants. Put cables in cable ducts or tape them to the walls higher up, remove chairs, and keep cupboard doors shut so your rabbit will not get trapped inside. Make sure you are always there to keep an eye on her.

Bunny Bathroom

Provide your rabbit with a place to go to the bathroom. You could use a litter box and fill it up with bedding, as well as a bit of soiled bedding from her cage so she recognizes the smell. If you see one of your rabbits suddenly stop, become tense, and lift her rear then quickly place her in

Do not forget to provide your rabbit with a nest box, even in her outdoor playpen, so she has somewhere to hide.

her litter box. If she goes to the bathroom in the right place, praise her and give her a treat. She will quickly learn where to go.

Accidents

If your rabbit urinates or leaves her droppings on the floor, do not yell at her because she will get scared. The droppings can be easily swept up and any urine puddles can be wiped up with a damp cloth and hot, soapy water.

Dangers on the Balcony

In most cases, balconies are unfortunately not suitable for rabbits. They are either too hot or too drafty, the floor is too slippery, and the railings are dangerous for rabbits because they could get their heads stuck in betweeen them. If your rabbit needs some fresh air, you could put her cage out on the balcony, but do not place the cage in direct sunlight or drafts. Also make sure there is not too great a temperature difference between outside and inside.

The Rabbit-Proof Balcony

You can quite easily bunny-proof your balcony. Cover holes in the railings with mesh wire or wooden boards. Lay down straw mats on the cold, slippery floor, but bear in mind these may get eaten! If you take these steps to make your balcony safe for your rabbit, you can now let her explore. But do not leave her alone! Cats or birds of prey could strike at any moment, so you may also need roof netting as well.

Vacationing at Home

Before you let your rabbit run around in the yard, slowly get her accustomed to eating fresh grass.

Fresh grass under her paws, sun on her fur, and plenty of weeds to nibble on— being outdoors is a true treat for a rabbit. Build her a pen and let her spend lots of time outdoors when it is warm.

So the snow has melted, the first shoots are up, the air is warmer, and the sun is shining. Everyone wants to be outdoors— and that includes your rabbit. If possible, treat your pet to this pleasure on a regular basis. Your rabbit will love to be outdoors and stimulate her senses! If the ground is dry and it is at least 64°F, then it is time to go outside! So your rabbit does not get indigestion, get her used to eating grass before she goes outside.

Fun in the Sun

Take your rabbit's playpen out on the lawn. Make sure she has hay, water, and a nest box, and also use an umbrella or some sort of cover to provide shade if the sun is beaming down. Sit next to her in a deck chair and enjoy yourselves. Keep an eye on her though to make sure she does not start digging!

Champion Diggers

Rabbits are world-champion diggers. She can dig an escape tunnel in no time when she is out in the pen, and she will soon be happily hopping free around the yard before you know it! This could put your bunny at risk. She could run away or be attacked by predators.

Do Not Let Her Loose in the Yard!

Tip

No matter how tame your rabbits are, never let them loose in the yard without an outdoor enclosure. Otherwise they may escape and never come back.

Outdoor Enclosure

Your rabbit will be able to enjoy herself more if she has a large outdoor enclosure, such as a playpen. There are many types available in pet supply stores. You can also buy nets or covers to put over them for added protection against predators. The best option is a solid enclosure with a wire mesh roof so that predators cannot get in. A neighbor's cat may think it is great fun to hunt your rabbit, but your rabbit will not enjoy this at all!

Treat for the Senses

When she is outside, your rabbit can race around, nibble on grass or weeds, or simply lie in the sun. To make it even more entertaining, you could add tubes for her to hide in or branches for her to nibble on.

Outdoor Rabbits

Animal welfare organizations such as the ASPCA and the House Rabbit Society do not recommend keeping pet rabbits outdoors on a permanent basis. There are too many risks. The most obvious danger is attack from predators, such as cats, dogs, raccoons, opossums, owls, and hawks, especially at night when there are no humans around to keep watch. No matter how secure the enclosure seems to be, a hungry hunter can tear into the hutch or possibly figure out how to open the cage door. Another reason not to house your rabbit outside is exposure to the elements. You would not want to be stuck outdoors in extreme weather, would you? Neither does your rabbit! Do not let your rabbit go outside if it is too hot, too cold, raining, snowing, or storming. Another outdoor hazard is poisonous plants that may be growing in your yard. Despite what many people think, domesticated animals do not instinctively avoid eating things that are bad for them. Another point to keep in mind is that most outdoor rabbits are not as tame as rabbits that live indoors. In short, indoor rabbits live longer, healthier lives than outdoor rabbits.

→ *Examples of Poisonous Plants in the House and Yard*

agave	cotoneaster	geraniums	monkshood	sage
aloe vera	crocus	goldenchain tree	myrtle	scotch broom
amaryllis	croton	hemlock	oleander	spurge
angel trumpet	crown-of-thorns	holly	Oregon-grape	tiger lily
anthurium	cuckoopint	honeysuckle	parsnip	tomato
azaleas	cyclamen	hyacinth	peony	tulip
bush lily	daffodils	hydrangea	periwinkle	venus flytrap
butterfly weed	daphne	iris	poinsettia	violet
calla	datura	ivy	poison ivy	Virginia creeper
castor	dieffenbachia	lantana	pothos	wisteria
cherry laurel	Easter lily	lily of the valley	primrose	yew
Christmas rose	ferns	lupine	privet	
chrysanthemum	fig tree	mistletoe	rhododendron	

An Adventure Playground for Rabbits

Running around the house will be great fun for your rabbit, but sooner or later he is going to know every nook and cranny—so now it is time to add a little more variety. Using simple objects and accessories, you can create an exciting adventure playground for your rabbit that will encourage him to explore again and again. Do not use all the new ideas at once. It is better to provide him with something new from time to time.

Burrowers

Rabbits love to investigate small spaces. Give him clay, cork, or wooden pipes that have an entrance and exit at both ends; baskets and boxes made of straw; or simply a new nest box for him to hide in.

Dark holes and small entrances are irresistible to rabbits. Each one must be investigated right away!

Tubes also make good viewing platforms.

Climbing

Rabbits love to climb, and everything they can crawl into they will try to climb on as well. You will soon see your rabbit exploring his new toys. You could even make a staircase out of bricks for him to climb up.

Fun Indoors and Outdoors — *Tip*

You can use any of these adventure playground objects either indoors or outdoors. But do not forget to put away any materials overnight that could be ruined outside, such as cardboard boxes or anything made of straw.

Or you could put the nest box on some bricks and use a small board as a steep ramp so he can climb up and use it as an observation point. One great thing about all this climbing is that it will wear down his claws.

Rabbits are champion diggers. Give your rabbit a box filled with sand or old rags so he can dig to his heart's content.

Jungle Expedition

Grab a bunch of leafy branches. The best ones are unfertilized fruit, beech, or hazel trees. Lay them around the room. Now he has his own jungle! Your rabbit can climb over the branches, hide in them, or nibble on the leaves and bark.

Digging Fun

For this, you will need a box and some sand. Fill up the box with sand and place it in the middle of the room. Your rabbit will love this and dig enthusiastically in the sand. But be aware that the sand will not stay in the box for very long! This is more suitable for outdoors because he will make quite a mess. However, there is an indoor alternative: use a box with high sides or just fill a box with old rags (be careful that he does not get his claws tangled up in them though).

Finding Food to Stay Fit

A rabbit will love finding tasty treats hidden around him. So you could fill your adventure playground with little goodies for him. For example:

→ Do not just fill his bowl with dry food—hide some throughout the room.

→ Fill a basket with hay and then hide bits of vegetables inside.

→ Tie a bunch of parsley together and hang it up so your rabbit has to stretch up to reach it.

→ Jam a piece of carrot in his cage bars to encourage him to stretch up and eat it.

→ You could hide treats under a small cardboard box. Your rabbit is guaranteed to show his creativity in getting to these treats!

→ Put some hay in a toilet tissue tube so he has to work to pull it out.

A Rabbit Circus

Rabbits Are Very Clever Animals!

Are you excited to show everyone what your rabbit can do? Then train your pet using these tricks so he can put on his best circus performance.

Walk the Tightrope

You need two bricks and a six-inch-wide board. Place the bricks a short width apart and use the board or plank to form a bridge. Use a treat to encourage your rabbit to walk across the bridge. Soon he will be doing it all by himself!

Hurdler

Lay out a few bricks and encourage your rabbit to jump over them by offering a treat. Use a command such as "Jump!" each time he does it.

Hoop Jump

Find a small hoop and get your rabbit to climb through it. Keep the hoop on the ground at first, and then slowly raise it higher and higher. How high can your rabbit jump?

Take a Bow

Rabbits are very good at stretching and reaching out for food. Place a treat in front of his nose and make him reach for it. This could be his farewell bow in his circus performance.

Rules of Play

To make sure your rabbit enjoys his circus performances, please follow these rules:

→ Do not make your rabbit do anything he does not want to do.

→ Reward him for every success with pats and treats.

→ Do not practice for too long or your rabbit will lose interest.

→ However, practice regularly so he does not forget all the tricks you have taught him.

→ The best time to train is in the early morning or evening, when he is feeling the most energetic. Do not disturb him if he is sleeping or eating.

Fun for All Ages

Brain Training for Smart Bunnies

Your rabbit is one lucky pet! She has a varied diet, lives in a large cage with plenty of room to move around, and has an exciting adventure playground to really let off some steam. Now let us find out how smart she is!

Through the Maze

Build a maze of cardboard boxes for your rabbit. It does not have to be very complex but should have at least one dead end. Now place a piece of food at one end, and watch your rabbit try to seek out the correct path. Does she get faster each time she does it? What happens if you

change the route? If you have more than one rabbit, which rabbit finds the food the fastest? Which one takes the longest?

The Bowl Trick

Get four bowls in different colors. Or attach a sticker or colored paper on four different bowls. Put food in one bowl only and cover the top. At first, of course, your rabbit will sniff out the food and go to the filled bowl. After you have done this a few times though, you will see she will walk toward the filled bowl without any hesitation, even if you swap around the bowls so they are in a different order.

Get four colorful bowls and put some food in the red one and cover it. How long will it take your rabbit to find the food?

Pretty Smart

Now try this: every time you feed your rabbits, give a whistle or ring a small bell while you put the food in the bowl. Your rabbits will soon come running to investigate because they will associate the noise with feeding time.

Training With Love

According to animal psychologists, animals will respond well to training if they are not afraid of their trainer. The animals must be treated with kindness and patience. Then, they will respond well and enjoy their training.

Plenty of Time for Play

You should spend as much time as possible with your rabbits, playing with them and cuddling them. Giving them new challenges will make them smarter and happier. Many different objects in their cage will keep their minds sharp and active. In return for your loving care, your rabbits will give you years of enjoyment, affection, and companionship.

Test

How Well Do You Know Your Rabbits?

And now it is time for a test: How well do you know your rabbits? And how well do your rabbits know you?

- [ ] My rabbits hop toward me if they see me coming.

- [ ] If I offer them something delicious, my rabbits immediately come running up to me.

- [ ] I know exactly what makes my rabbits the most curious.

- [ ] I know exactly what makes my rabbits afraid.

- [ ] My rabbits love to be stroked and enjoy cuddles.

- [ ] My rabbits have a chance to exercise every day, with plenty of new adventures and objects.

- [ ] My rabbits love to investigate new toys and exercise equipment.

- [ ] When I rustle my hand in the bag of hay, my rabbits come up to me and watch me.

- [ ] If I hide treats inside the cage, my rabbits immediately look for them.

Have you answered yes to all these statements? Congratulations! You and your rabbits make a great team!

Understanding Your Rabbit

The Senses

Sight

Rabbits have an almost 360-degree view of movements and can see well, even in twilight. They see the world in color although they cannot differentiate between red and green.

Hearing

Rabbits have very good hearing, and their ears are like little satellite dishes they can move in all directions, independently of one another. They are very sensitive to loud noises.

Smell

Rabbits have super noses! A large part of their communication depends on scent messages. Strong smells such as cleaning products or cigarette smoke are very strong to a rabbit.

Taste

Rabbits are gourmets. They like a varied diet and have their own individual likes and dislikes.

Touch

They can find their way around in the dark with their sensitive whiskers.

Exercise Is Essential

→ Rabbits have an urge to move around a lot and need exercise in order to stay healthy.

→ Even if your rabbit has a large cage, she should be allowed out of her cage for at least two or three hours a day.

→ Get rid of any dangerous objects before you let your rabbit out!

→ Always give her something new to investigate. Whether it is a new object or a hidden treat, keep things interesting for her.

→ Always make sure she has fresh water and hay available when she is on the move. Also, provide her with a nest box so she has somewhere to hide.

→ If your rabbit is going out in the yard, make sure she is used to eating grass first. Provide her with a stable enclosure with plenty of shade, and never leave her alone. This way you can keep an eye on the neighbor's cat, and also make sure your rabbit does not escape!

Adventure Playground

→ Clay, wooden, or cork pipes are ideal for your rabbit to climb in and out of.

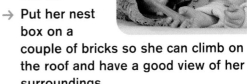

→ Put her nest box on a couple of bricks so she can climb on the roof and have a good view of her surroundings.

→ Give her branches or twigs to nibble on.

→ A sandbox will satisfy her need to dig.

→ Put treats high up so she has to reach for them.

→ Lie on the floor so your rabbit can climb all over you and investigate you, and perhaps have a cuddle with her. The more contact you have with your rabbit, the more loving she will be.

Translated from the German edition by Claire Mullen.

Edited and produced by Enslow Publishers, Inc.

Originally published in German.

© 2007 Franckh-Kosmos Verlags-GmbH & Co. KG, Stuttgart, Germany
Angela Beck, *Zwergkaninchen*

Library of Congress Cataloging-in-Publication Data

Beck, Angela.
  [Zwergkaninchen. English]
  Rabbits : keeping and caring for your pet / Angela Beck.
    pages cm. — (Keeping and caring for your pet)
  Audience: 11-up.
  Audience: Grade 7 to 8.
  Summary: "Discusses how to choose and care for a rabbit, including diet, behaviors, housing, grooming, exercise, popular breeds, and vet care"—Provided by publisher.
  Includes bibliographical references and index.
  ISBN 978-0-7660-4183-7
  1. Rabbits—Juvenile literature. I. Title.
  SF453.2.B43 2013
  636.932'2—dc23
                          2012041568

Paperback ISBN 978-1-4644-0297-5

Printed in the United States of America

052013 Lake Book Manufacturing, Inc., Melrose Park, IL

10 9 8 7 6 5 4 3 2 1

To Our Readers: We have done our best to make sure all Internet addresses in this book were active and appropriate when we went to press. However, the author and publisher have no control over and assume no liability for the material available on those Internet sites or on other Web sites they may link to. Any comments or suggestions can be sent by e-mail to comments@enslow.com or to the address on the back cover.

Every effort has been made to locate all copyright holders of material used in this book. If any errors or omissions have occurred, corrections will be made in future editions of this book.

All information in this book is given to the best of the author's knowledge. However, care during implementation is still required. The publishers, authors, and translators assume no liability for personal injury, property damage, or financial loss as a result of the application of the methods and ideas presented in this book.

✪ Enslow Publishers, Inc., is committed to printing our books on recycled paper. The paper in every book contains 10% to 30% post-consumer waste (PCW). The cover board on the outside of each book contains 100% PCW. Our goal is to do our part to help young people and the environment too!

Photo Credits: Color photos taken by Ulrike Schanz especially for the purposes of this book except Juniors Bildarchiv, pp. 8, 9, 10 (gray rabbit); Shutterstock, p. 1.

Cover Photos: *Main photo:* Eric Isselée/Photos.com (tan and white lop). *Bottom, from left to right:* Shutterstock.com (gray rabbit, brown lop, white rabbit, white and gray rabbit). *Back:* Ulrike Schanz (author photo); Shutterstock.com (black and white rabbit).

Index

Further Reading

Books

Biniok, Janice. *Rabbits.* Pittsburgh, Penn.: Eldorado Ink, 2009.

Mead, Marie, and Nancy Laroche. *Rabbits: Gentle Hearts, Valiant Spirits.* Charlottesville, Va.: Nova Maris Press, 2011.

Parker, Karen. *The Rabbit Handbook.* Hauppauge, N.Y.: Barron's Educational Series, 2009.

Russell, Geoff. *Mini Encyclopedia of Rabbit Breeds and Care: A Color Directory of the Most Popular Breeds and Their Care.* Buffalo, N.Y.: Firefly Books, 2009.

Internet Addresses

House Rabbit Society
http://www.rabbit.org

ASPCA: General Rabbit care
http://www.aspca.org/pet-care/small-pet-care/general-rabbit-care.aspx

American Rabbit Breeders Association, Inc.
http://www.arba.net